AL LEONARD GUITAR METHOD BOOK 2

BY WILL SCHMID AND GREG KOCH

ISBN 0-634-01313-0

HAL•LEONARD® CORPORATION

7777 W. BLUEMOUND RD. P.O. BOX 13819 MILWAUKEE, WI 53213

Visit Hal Leonard Online at
www.halleonard.com

THE Am CHORD

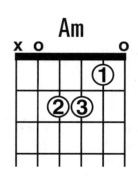

Am

Practice changing chords in the following examples. Play slowly and steadily so there is no hesitation between chords.

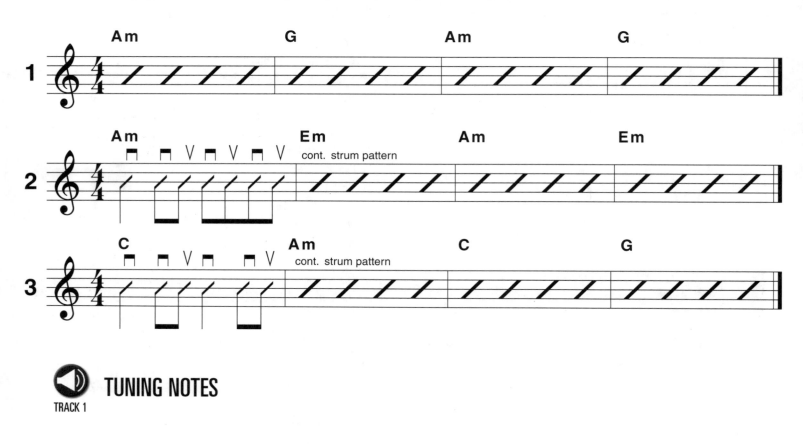

1. | Am | G | Am | G |

2. | Am | Em | Am | Em |
   cont. strum pattern

3. | C | Am | C | G |
   cont. strum pattern

TUNING NOTES

TRACK 1

TRACK 2

SINNER MAN

Traditional

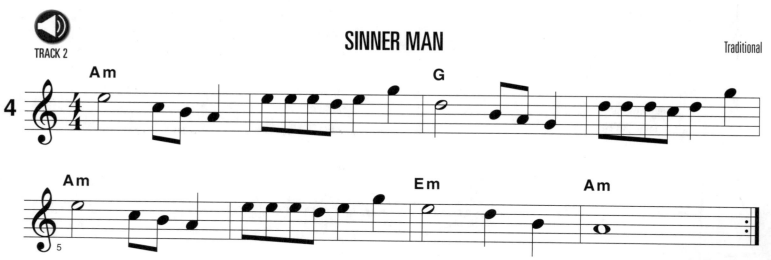

DOTTED QUARTER NOTES

You've already learned that a dot after a note increases the value by one half.

$$\text{♩ (2 beats)} + \text{. (1 beat)} = \text{♩. (3 beats)}$$

A dot after a quarter note also increases its value by one half.

$$\text{♩ (1 beat)} + \text{. (½ beat)} = \text{♩. (1½ beats)}$$

Practice the riffs below, which use dotted quarter notes.

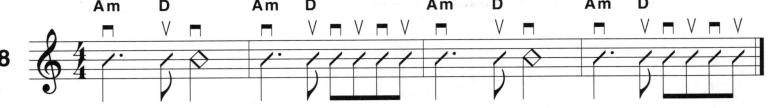

787.87 Sc
Schmid, Will.
Hal Leonard guitar method

THE Dm CHORD

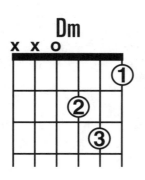

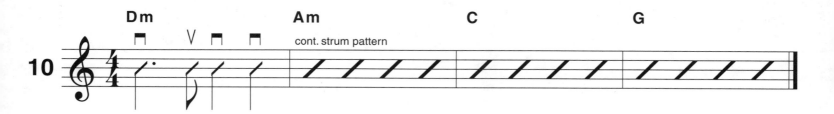

EIGHTH REST

The equivalent rest for an eighth note looks like this:

$$\eighthnote = \quad \gamma$$

You can either lift your left-hand fingers off the chord or dampen the strings with your right hand.

SYNCOPATION

Syncopation is the stressing or accenting of notes on the "ands" of beats. The accent may be a result of tying eighth notes together or of placing quarter notes on the off-beats.

Use alternate picking throughout the following exercises. When you see a count in parentheses, simply miss the string and let the sound ring. By doing this you will play the syncopated pattern with the correct stroke of the pick.

Following are two common syncopated strum patterns. Practice these with various chords.

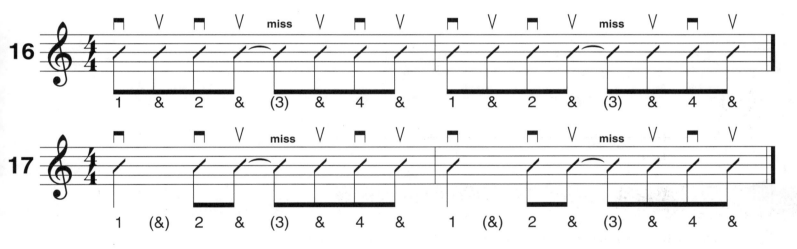

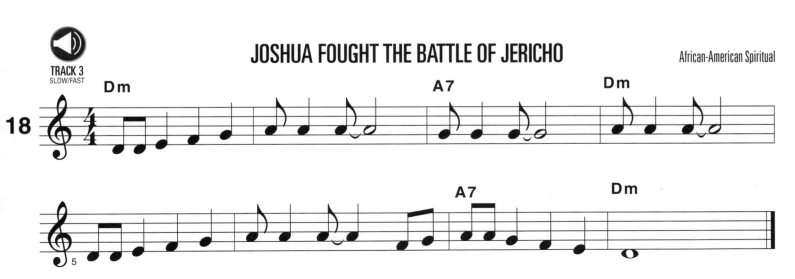

TRACK 3
SLOW/FAST

JOSHUA FOUGHT THE BATTLE OF JERICHO

African-American Spiritual

5

First play the melody; then sing as you strum the chords for the next song.

ROCK-A-MY SOUL

African-American Spiritual

TRACK 4
SLOW/FAST

19

Rock - a - my soul in the bos - om of A - bra - ham,

rock - a - my soul in the bos - om of A - bra - ham, rock - a - my soul in the

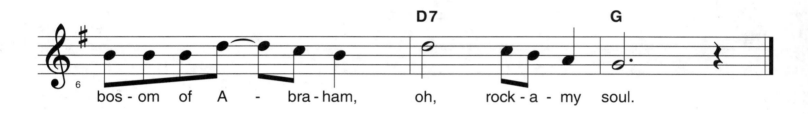

bos - om of A - bra - ham, oh, rock - a - my soul.

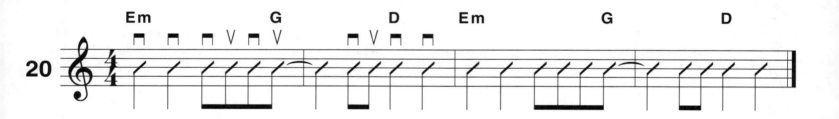

20

Release your left-hand pressure when an eighth rest is indicated in the next example.

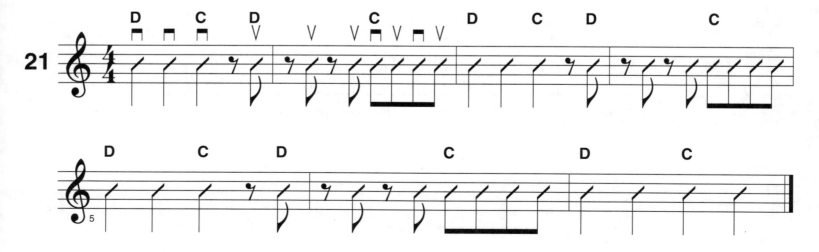

21

22

23

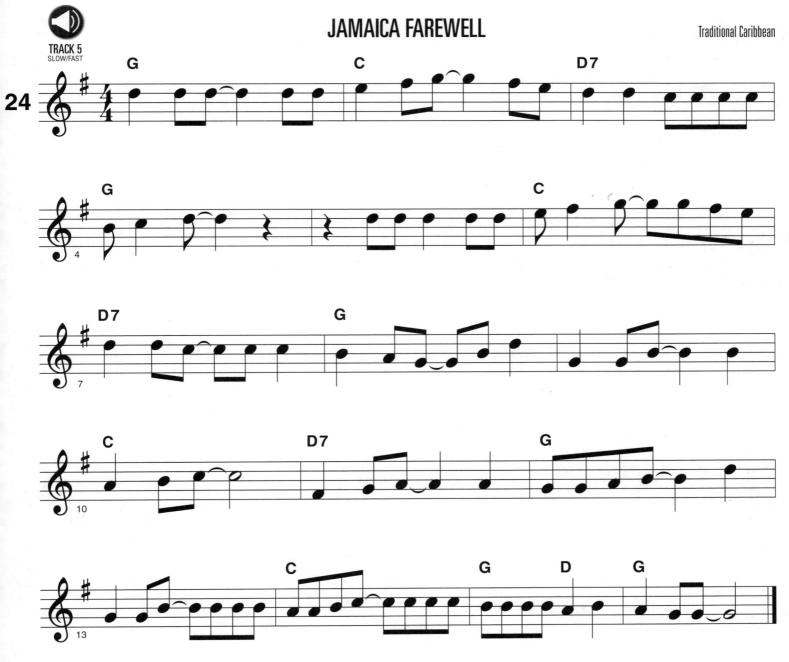

JAMAICA FAREWELL

Traditional Caribbean

THE A CHORD

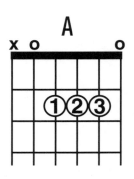

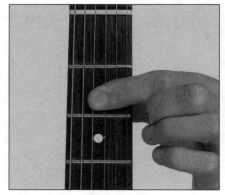

Optional Fingering (string 1 is not played)

On the next example, try muting the strings on each rest with your left-hand fingers.

Here is another type of muting effect. As you strum the muted chord (X), touch the strings with your palm a split second before you strike them with your pick.

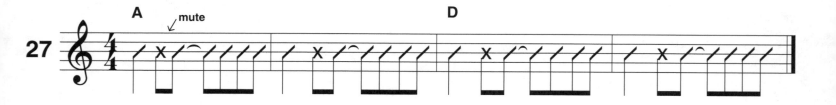

WHAT'S A KEY

The **key** is another name for a tonal center of a song. Songs usually end on their key note. So far, you have played in the keys of C (no sharps of flats) and G (one sharp).

THE KEY OF D

The key signature for D has an F-sharp and a C-sharp. All Fs and Cs should be played one half step (fret) higher.

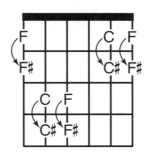

TRACK 6

OH, MARY DON'T YOU WEEP

Traditional Spiritual

Verse

28

If I could I sure - ly would, __ stand on the rock where the Mo-ses stood. __

Pha-raoh's ar - my got __ drown - ded, oh, Ma - ry don't you weep.

Chorus

Oh, Ma - ry don't you weep, don't you mourn, Oh, Ma - ry don't you weep, don't you mourn.

Pha-raoh's ar - my got __ drown - ded, oh, Ma - ry don't you weep.

FOURTH FINGER WORKOUT

Build up the muscles in your fourth finger by playing these exercises.

A **natural** sign (♮) cancels a sharp in the key signature for the remainder of the measure.

DE COLORES

Mexican Folk Song

TRACK 7

29

All _____ the col-ors, all the col-ors that bloom in the
De _____ co - lo-res, de co - lo-res se vis-ten los

mead-ows are col-ors of spring-time. _____
cam-pos en la pri-ma - ve - ra. _____

All _____ the col-ors, all the col-ors that dance in the
De _____ co - lo-res, de co - lo-res son los pa-ja-

sky are the col-ors of rain-bows. _____
ri-tos que vie-nen de a fue-ra. _____

All _____ the col-ors, all the col-ors of na-ture spring
De _____ co - lo-res, de co - lo-res es el ar-co

forth to make my heart sing. Then I know why the col-ors of
i-ris que ve-mos lu - cir, y por e - so los gran-des a-

spring-time are bring-ing me joy and a heart full of love.
mo - res de mu-chos co - lo-res me gus-tan a mí.

ENDINGS

The following song has a first and second ending indicated by brackets with the numbers 1 and 2.

When you reach the repeat sign (:||) in the first ending, go back to the beginning. On the second time through, skip the first ending and go on to the second ending.

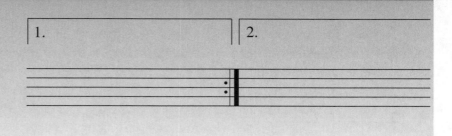

TRACK 8

ANGELS WE HAVE HEARD ON HIGH

Traditional French Carol

An - gels we have heard on high sweet - ly sing - ing o'er the plains,

and the moun - tains in re - ply ech - o - ing their joy - ous strains.

Glo - ri - a

1. in ex - cel - sis de - o, 2. in ex - cel - sis de - o.

TRACK 9
SLOW/FAST

CATCHY RIFF

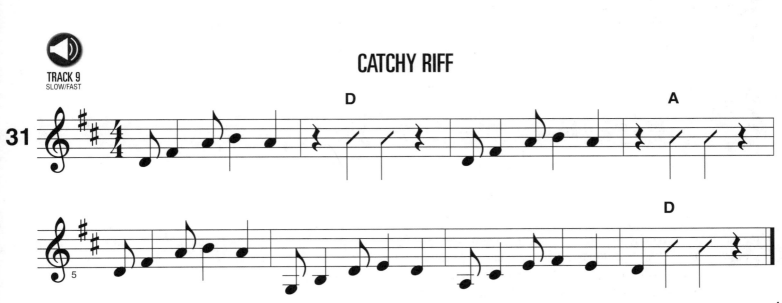

SECOND POSITION

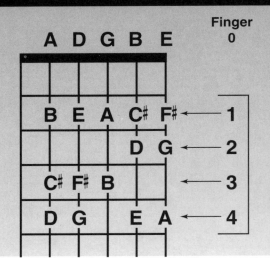

Finger
0

Throughout Book 1 and until now in Book 2 you have played in **first position**, with the first finger in the first fret, the second finger in the second fret, and so on. The name of your finger position is determined by where you place your first finger.

If the first finger is placed at the second fret as indicated by the diagram at the left, you will be playing in what is called **second position**. Fingers 2, 3, and 4 play in frets 3, 4, and 5 as indicated.

Notice that open notes can also be played in an alternate position on the fretboard.

The principal advantage of playing in the second position lies in the ease with which certain passages can be fingered.

Practice the song below in second position using both the open-string notes and their alternate fingerings on the fretboard.

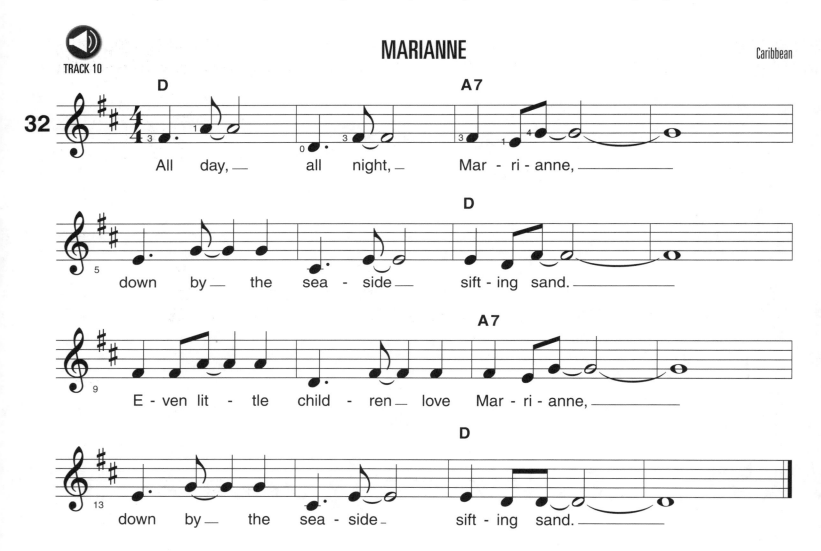

MARIANNE

Caribbean

TRACK 10

After playing the melody to "Marianne," try playing some of the syncopated strums you've already learned. You can also go back to pages 10 and 11 and play those melodies in second position.

Some songs are played in more than one position. The following piece shifts between first position and second position.

BLUES/ROCK RIFF

TRACK 11

THE HIGH A NOTE

Play the new note, A, with your fourth finger in second position.

THE WABASH CANNONBALL

TRACK 12

Hobo Song

Lis - ten to the jin - gle, the rum - ble and the roar.

Rid - ing through the wood - lands to the hills and by the shore. Hear the

might - y rush of the en - gine, hear the lone - some ho - bo squall.

Rid - ing through the jun - gle on the Wa - bash Can - non - ball.

THE E CHORD

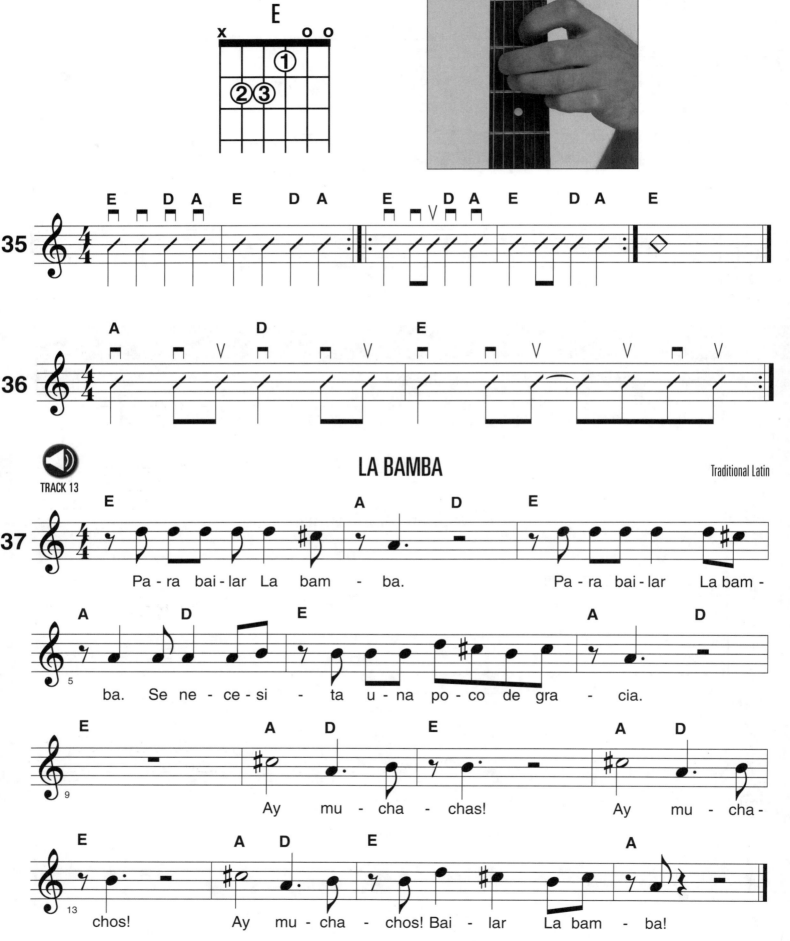

LA BAMBA

Traditional Latin

Pa - ra bai - lar La bam - ba. Pa - ra bai - lar La bam -

ba. Se ne - ce - si - ta u - na po - co de gra - cia.

Ay mu - cha - chas! Ay mu - cha -

chos! Ay mu - cha - chos! Bai - lar La bam - ba!

THE KEY OF A

The key signature for A has three sharps: F-sharp, C-sharp, and G-sharp. Study the diagram below to learn where the new G♯ notes are played.

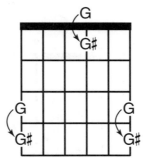

Play "Joy to the World" in second position.

POWER CHORDS

The **power chord** is commonly used in rock and other contemporary music. Most chords have three or more notes; power chords have just two. Also, notice that power chords are labeled with the suffix "5."

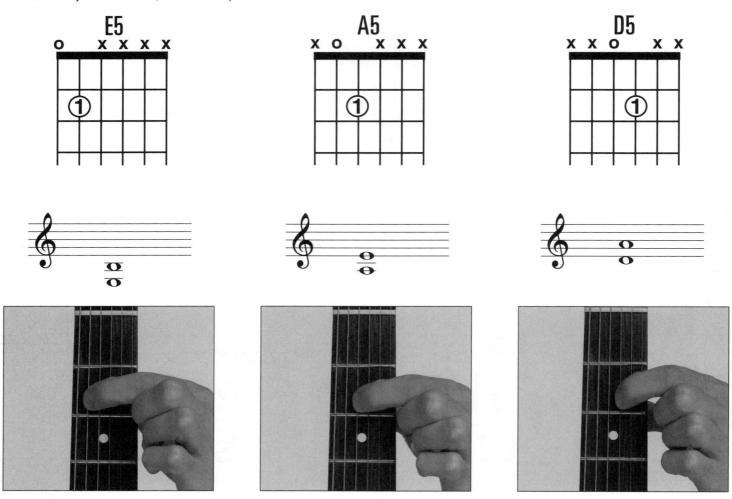

TABLATURE

Tablature graphically represents the guitar fingerboard. Each horizontal line represents a string, and each number represents a fret.

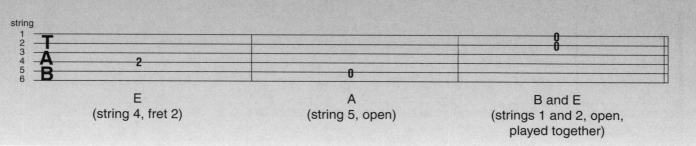

The same information is given on the musical staff and in tablature. Practice reading both.

TRACK 15
SLOW/FAST

STEADY GROOVE

THE SHUFFLE

In traditional styles like blues and jazz, eighth notes are played unevenly. Play the first note twice as long as the second.

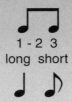

Playing the eighth notes in this way will give you the desired shuffle or "swing" feel.

POWER CHORD SHUFFLE

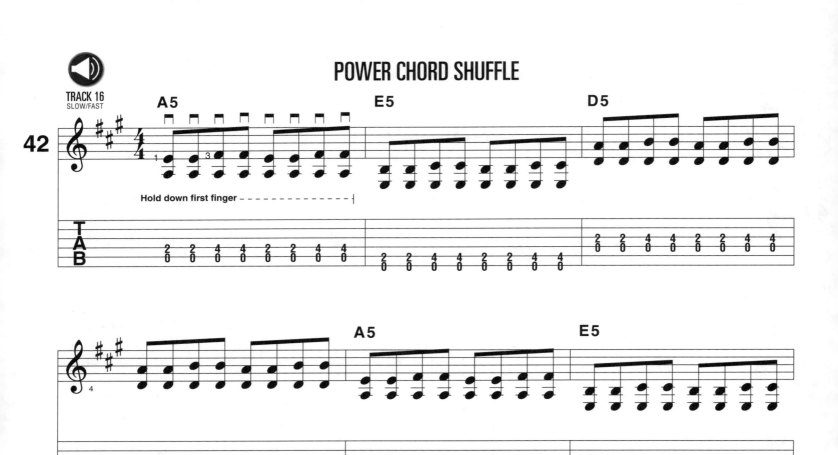

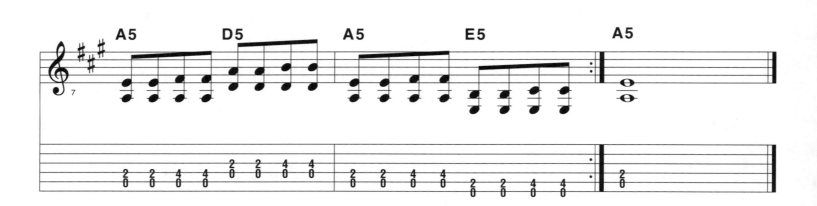

Practice the following song using the power chord shuffle accompaniment you just learned. Or, play the melody using the shuffle rhythm.

MIDNIGHT SPECIAL

Prison Song

TRACK 17

Verse

Well you wake up in the morn - ing, — hear the ding - dong ring, — Go march - ing to the ta - ble, — see the same darn thing, Knife and fork are on the ta - ble — noth - in' in my pan, — And if you say a thing a - bout it, — you're in trou - ble with the

Chorus

man. Let the mid - night spe - cial, — shine its light on — you. — Let the mid - night spe - cial — shine its ev - er lov - in' light on you.

Try playing "Midnight Special" again using an even eighth note rock feel.

TRACK 18

THE BLUES

The blues style was originated in the early 1900s by African Americans from the Mississippi Delta. Blues became an important ingredient in jazz, country, rock, and other forms of popular music.

The most typical blues is twelve measures (bars) long. Many **12-bar blues** follow this chord progression below. Use the power chord shuffle you have just learned.

SHUFFLE RIFF

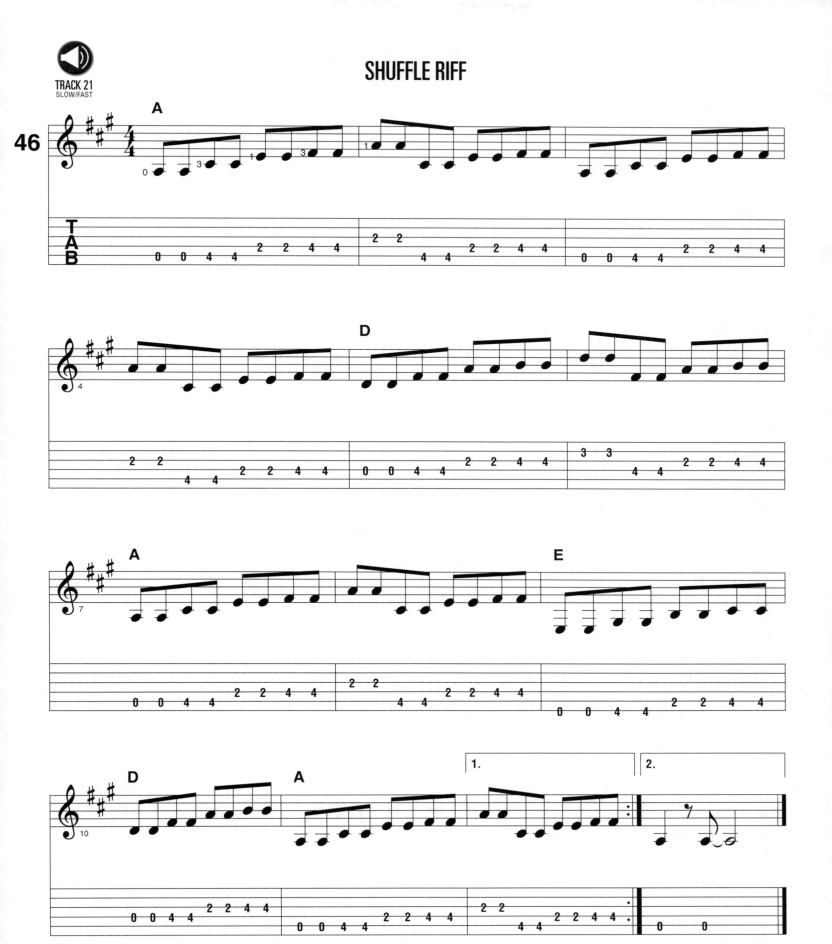

THE KEY OF Am

The **key of A minor** has a key signature of no sharps or flats. A minor is called the **relative minor** of C major because it shares the same parent key signature. The relative minor always begins two notes lower than the major key (C-B-A).

"Wayfaring Stranger" is a well-known Sacred Harp spiritual from the Southern United States.

WAYFARING STRANGER

Sacred Harp Spiritual

TRACK 22

When a G# is added to A natural minor, it is called the **harmonic minor**. Find all of the G# notes (one fret higher than G or one fret lower than A) before playing "Hava Nagila." Notice that "Hava Nagila" speeds up on the repeat then slows down on the last line.

HAVA NAGILA

Israeli Dance

TRACK 23

Ha - va na - gi - la, ha - va na - gi - la, ha - va na - gi - la, vay nis - m' - cha.

Ha - va na - gi - la, ha - va na - gi - la, ha - va na - gi - la, vay nis - m' - cha.

Ha - va n' ra - ne - nah, ha - va n' ra - ne - nah, ha - va n' ra - ne - nah vay nis - m' - cha.

Ha - va n' ra - ne - nah, ha - va n' ra - ne - nah, ha - va n'-ra - ne - nah, vay nis - m' - cha.

U - ru, u - ru a - chim, u - rua chim b' lev - sa me - ach,

u - rua- chim b' lev - sa me - ach, u - rua- chim b' lev - sa me - ach, u - rua - chim b' lev - sa me - ach,

U - rua - chim, u - rua - chim, b' lev - sa me - ach.

23

FINGERSTYLE GUITAR

Fingerstyle, also known as fingerpicking, is a very popular style of guitar accompaniment which uses **arpeggios** (broken chords) instead of strummed chords. The distinctive sound of fingerpicking comes from the thumb and fingers plucking only one string each in succession.

The right-hand finger and thumb letters used in this book are based on the internationally accepted system of Spanish words and letters:

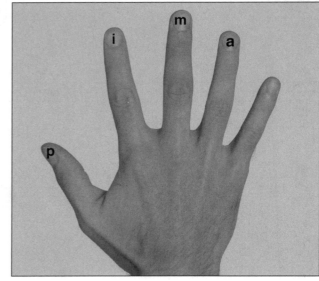

p	pulgar	=	thumb
i	indice	=	index finger
m	medio	=	middle finger
a	anular	=	ring finger

Follow these steps to learn how to fingerpick:

- The thumb (p) plucks strings 4, 5, and 6 depending upon which string is the bass or root of the chord. This motion is a downward stroke. Use the left side of the thumb and thumbnail.

- The other fingers (i, m, a) pluck the string in an upward stroke with the fleshy tip of the finger and fingernail.

- The index finger (i) always plucks string 3.

- The middle finger (m) always plucks string 2.

- The ring finger (a) always plucks string 1.

The thumb and each finger must pluck only one string per stroke and not brush over several strings. (This would be a strum.) Let the strings ring throughout the duration of the chord.

RIGHT-HAND POSITION

Use a high wrist; arch your palm as if you were holding a ping-pong ball. Keep the thumb outside and away from the fingers, and let the fingers do the work rather than lifting your whole hand. Study the photo at the right.

Practice the fingerpicking patterns below. Work toward an even sound on each string plucked.

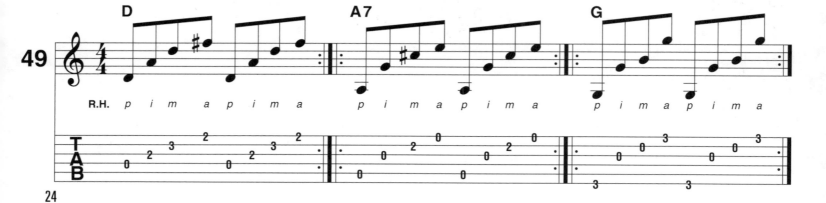

SWING LOW, SWEET CHARIOT

African-American Spiritual

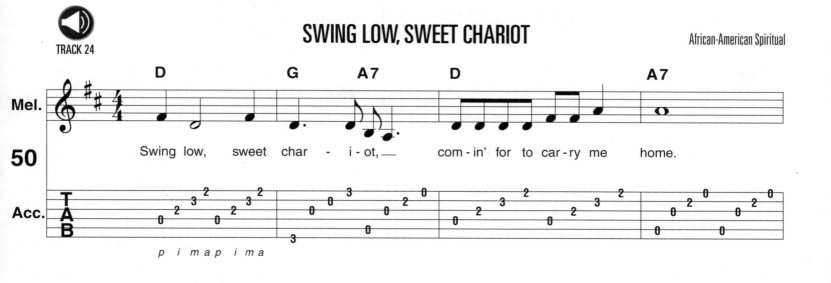

50

Swing low, sweet char - i - ot, — com - in' for to car - ry me home.

p i m a p i m a

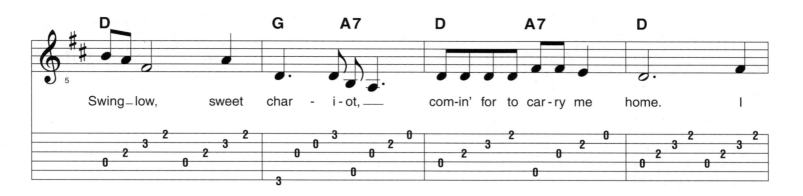

Swing low, sweet char - i - ot, — com - in' for to car - ry me home. I

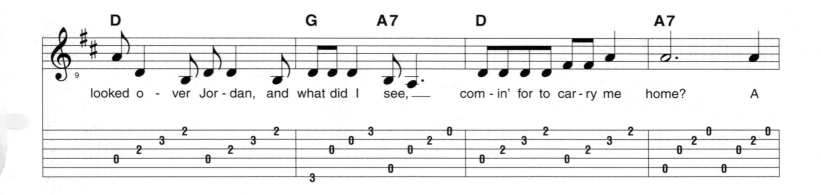

looked o - ver Jor - dan, and what did I see, — com - in' for to car - ry me home? A

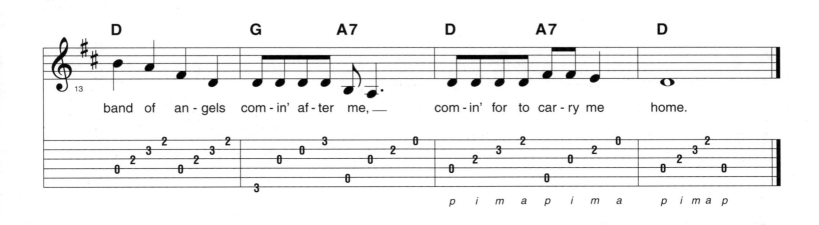

band of an - gels com - in' af - ter me, — com - in' for to car - ry me home.

p i m a p i m a p i m a p

The fingerstyle pattern used in "Scarborough Fair" is commonly used for songs in $\frac{3}{4}$ time.

SCARBOROUGH FAIR

British Ballad

The fingerstyle accompaniment to "The Water Is Wide" uses two new chords, **Bm/A** (B minor with an A in the bass) and **Dadd9** (D with an open first string) that are easy to play. Study each chord frame below before playing the accompaniment.

THE WATER IS WIDE

English Folk Song

THE F CHORD

Unlike other chords you have played, the F chord has two strings depressed by one finger. The first finger forms a small **barre** across strings 1 and 2. You will find that it is easier to roll this finger slightly so that the strings are depressed by the outside rather than the flat underside of the first finger.

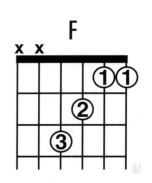

Another option for playing arpeggios is to use a pick. Try this on the next song.

PICKING CHORDS

TRACK 27

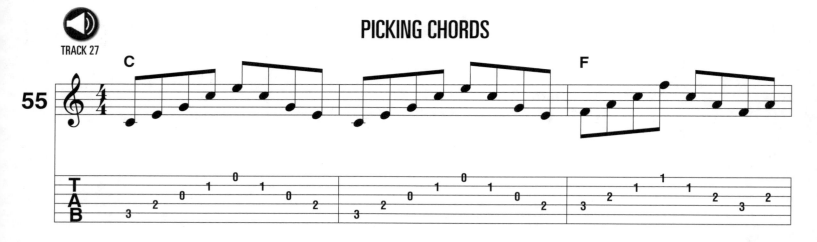

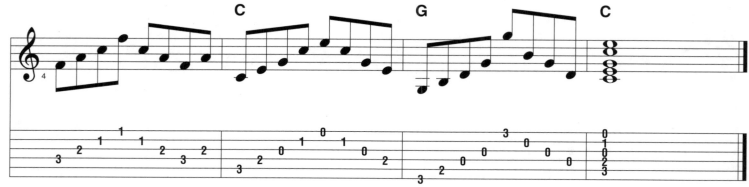

Play the accompaniment to "House of the Rising Sun" either with a pick or fingerstyle.

HOUSE OF THE RISING SUN

American Ballad

CARTER STYLE SOLOS

Carter style solos are a famous guitar style popularized by Country music legend Maybelle Carter of the Carter family. The melody is played on the lower strings and the spaces between the melody are filled by strummed partial chords. Emphasize the melody notes and play lightly on the strums.

ROW, ROW, ROW YOUR BOAT

Traditional

MAN OF CONSTANT SORROW

Southern U.S. Ballad

WILDWOOD FLOWER

Appalachan Folk Song

BASS RUNS

A **bass run** is a pattern of notes that connects the bass notes of two chords. The bass run gives your accompaniment variety and provides momentum toward the new chord. Practice these bass runs between G and C or G and D; then play them with the bluegrass classic, "Goin' Down the Road."

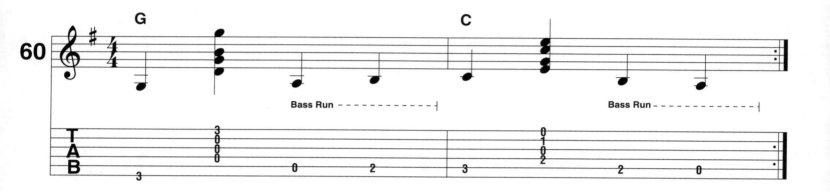

An optional form of the G to C run replaces the second beat strum with another bass note.

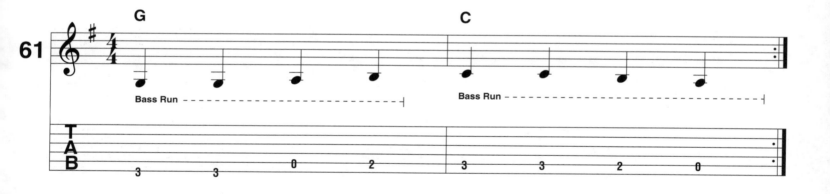

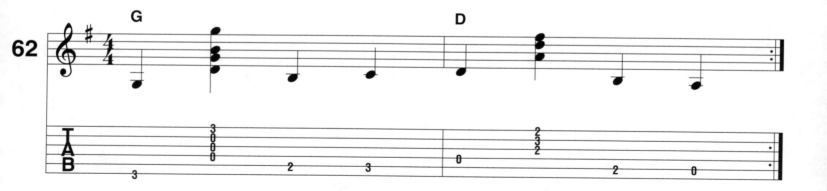

GOIN' DOWN THE ROAD

Bluegrass

2. I'm goin' where those chilly winds don't blow *(3 times)*
I ain't gonna be treated this a-way.

3. I'm goin' where the water tastes like wine *(3 times)*
I ain't gonna be treated this a-way.

THE B7 CHORD

B7 is your first four-finger chord. Notice that the second-fret fingers are placed on strings 1, 3, and 5. Keeping this visual pattern in mind will help you move to this chord quickly.

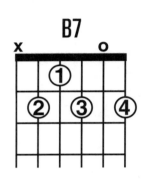

When you change from E or Em to B7, keep your second finger down.

TRACK 33

WE THREE KINGS

Traditional

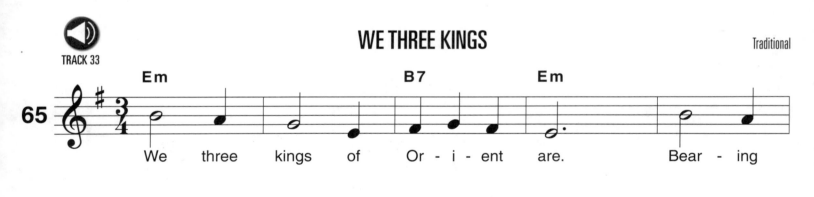

We three kings of Or - i - ent are. Bear - ing

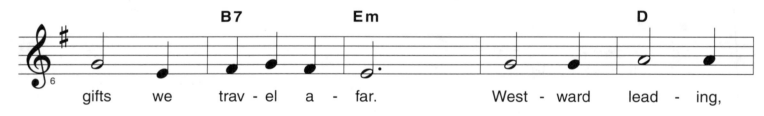

gifts we trav - el a - far. West - ward lead - ing,

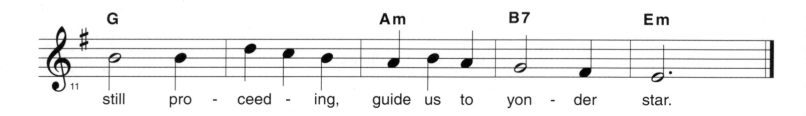

still pro - ceed - ing, guide us to yon - der star.

THE KEY OF E

On the guitar, the key of E sounds good. It is an ideal key for both singing and playing.

The key signature for E has four sharps: F-sharp, C-sharp, G-sharp, and D-sharp. Study the diagram below to learn where the new D# notes are played.

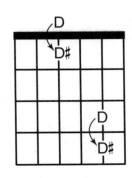

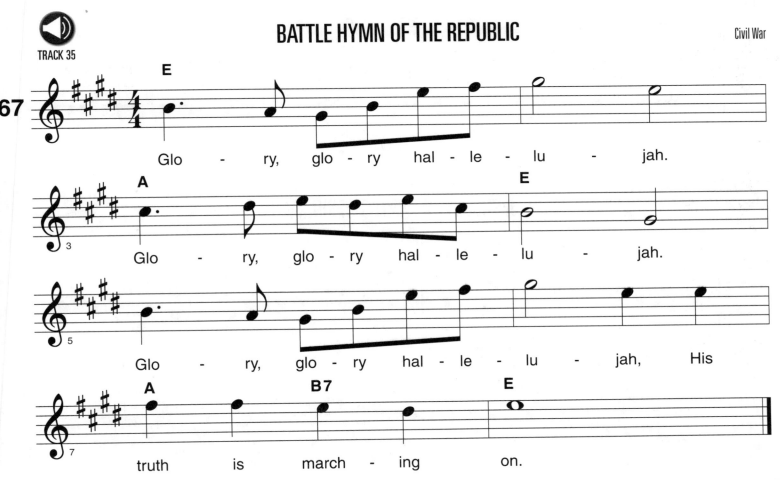

TRIPLETS

Triplets subdivide a unit into three parts instead of two parts. In $\frac{4}{4}$ or $\frac{3}{4}$ time, two eighth notes get one count, so an eight-note triplet will also get one count.

Triplets are beamed together with a number 3. To count a triplet, simply say the word "tri-pl-et" during one beat. Tap your foot to the beat, and count aloud:

COUNT: 1 2 tri - pi - let 4   tri - pi - let tri - pi - let 3   4   1   2   &   tri - pi - let 4

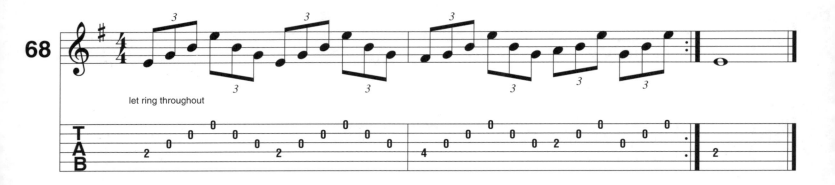

let ring throughout

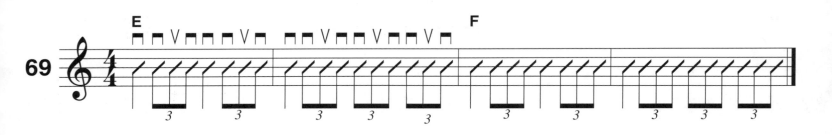

TRACK 36

JESU, JOY OF MAN'S DESIRING

Bach

DEEP BLUES

Triplets can also be applied to a 12-bar blues. Play the following piece in second position.

LOST IN THE SHUFFLE

THE PENTATONIC SCALE

Pentatonic scales are widely used in styles ranging from blues, rock, and country to various world musics. The easiest pentatonic (five-note scale) to play on the guitar includes the notes E, G, A, B, and D. If you start this scale on E, it is called the E **minor pentatonic**. If you start it on G (relative major) it is called the G **major pentatonic**.

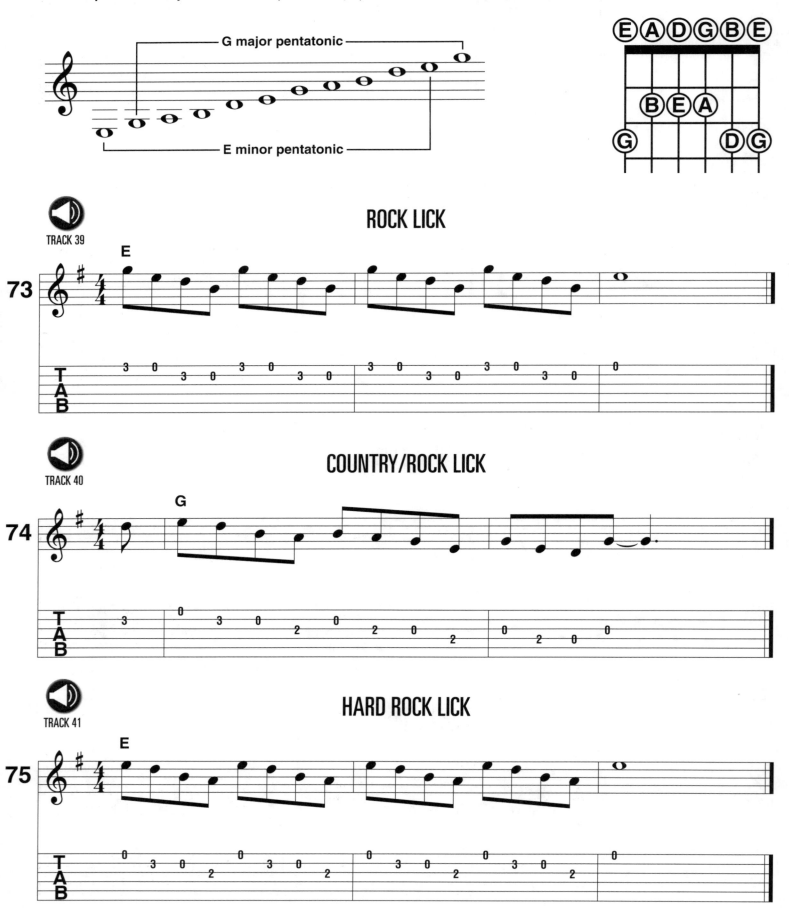

ROCK LICK

TRACK 39

COUNTRY/ROCK LICK

TRACK 40

HARD ROCK LICK

TRACK 41

BLUEGRASS LICK

COUNTRY LICK

BLUES LICK

ROCK 'N' ROLL LICK

BLUES/ROCK LICK

PENTATONIC LEAD GUITAR

IMPROVISING

Use the E minor pentatonic you just learned to play solo leads over a 12-bar blues in E. If you don't have the recording, take turns playing rhythm and leads with friends or record your own rhythm tracks and play lead over them.

IMPROV TIPS

- **Hang Around Home** – Base you solo around the root (letter name) of the chord being played.

- **Less Is More** – Choose your notes carefully; sometimes it's not the quantity it's the quality.

- **Work the Rhythm** – Use syncopations, triplets, and repeating patterns to help make your solos interesting and distinctive.

- **Tell a Story** – Let you solo take shape with a beginning, middle, and end.

TRACK 48

OPEN JAM

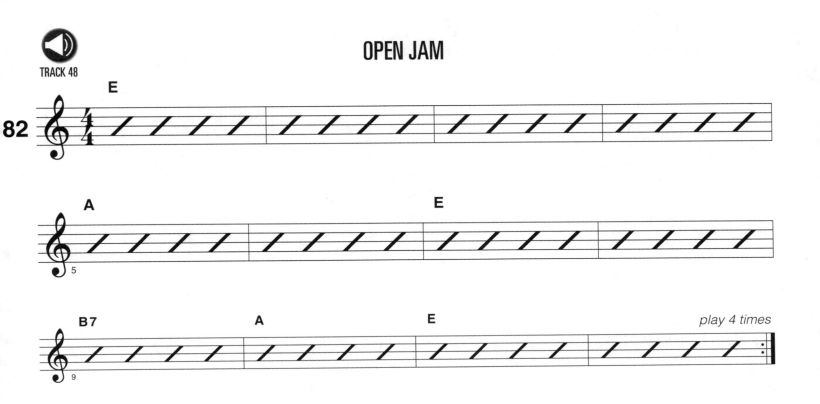

MOVABLE POWER CHORDS

So far, you have learned three power chords (E5, A5, and D5) that use an open string and first finger. Now use your first and third fingers to form a power chord that can be moved up and down the fingerboard.

The movable power chord shapes below are named by where the first finger is placed on the fretboard. You can use either strings 6 and 5 or strings 5 and 4 to play these chords.

SIXTH STRING ROOT

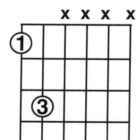

FIFTH STRING ROOT

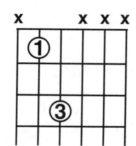

	E A
	F
	B
3rd Fret	G C
5th Fret	A D
7th Fret	B E
	C F
10th Fret	D G
12th Fret	E A

Study the fingerboard chart at the right to identify the letter names of natural notes on strings 6 and 5. If you want to play C5, locate C on either string 6 or string 5 and apply the correct shape from above. Move to D5 by simply sliding up two frets. That's the logic behind movable chords.

POP RIFF

TRACK 49

EARLY ROCK RIFF

TRACK 50

HARD ROCK RIFF

TRACK 51

POP/ROCK RIFF

TRACK 52

The next example uses both movable power chords and an open-position power chord you learned earlier in the book.

TRACK 53 **Shuffle**

ROCKABILLY RIFF

Now try two riffs that mix power chords with single notes.

TRACK 54

CLASSIC ROCK RIFF

TRACK 55

HEAVY ROCK RIFF

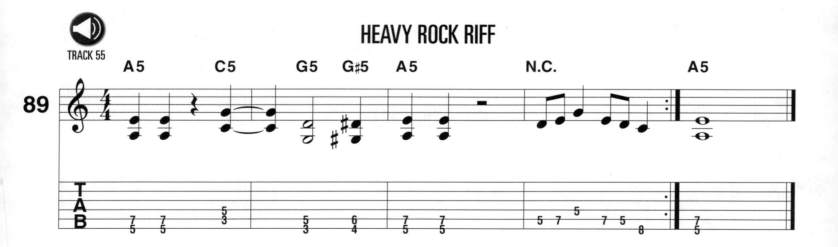

PALM MUTING

Palm muting is a technique in which you allow the side or heel of your picking hand to rest against the bridge, muffling or "muting" the strings as you play. Use this technique when you see the abbreviation "P.M." under the notes (between the staff and tab).

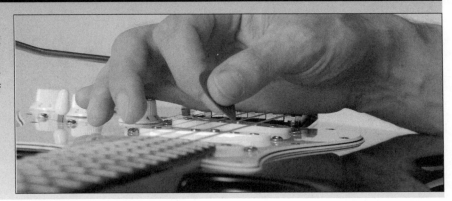

Palm muting sounds especially good with power chords and some amp distortion. Try this when playing the next two examples.

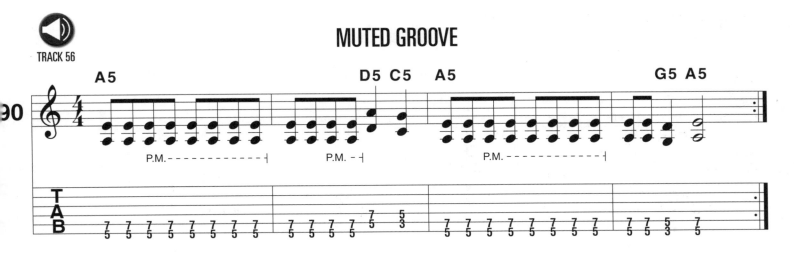

An **accent mark** (>) written above of below a note or chord indicates to play that note or chord slightly louder than the others.

GRAND FINALE

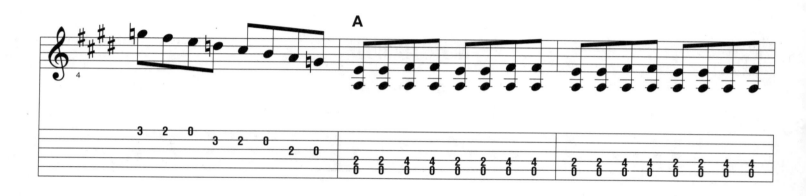

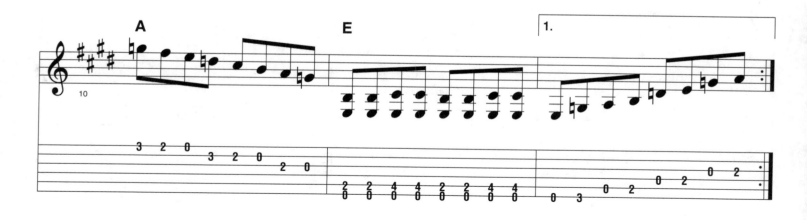

HAL LEONARD GUITAR METHOD

THE HAL LEONARD GUITAR METHOD is designed for anyone just learning to play acoustic or electric guitar. It is based on years of teaching guitar students of all ages, and it also reflects some of the best guitar teaching ideas from around the world.

This comprehensive method is preferred by teachers and students alike for many reasons:

- Learning sequence is carefully paced with clear instructions that make it easy to learn
- Popular songs increase the incentive to learn to play
- Versatile enough to be used as self-instruction or with a teacher
- Audio accompaniments let students have fun and sound great while practicing.